T0380722

THE
LITTLE
BOOK
OF
Jesus

GETTING TO KNOW GOD

JIM PRESTIDGE

WESTBOW
PRESS®
A DIVISION OF THOMAS NELSON
& ZONDERVAN

WestBow Press books may be ordered through booksellers or by contacting:

WestBow Press
A Division of Thomas Nelson & Zondervan
1663 Liberty Drive
Bloomington, IN 47403
www.westbowpress.com
844-714-3454

Because of the dynamic nature of the Internet, any web addresses or
links contained in this book may have changed since publication and
may no longer be valid. The views expressed in this work are solely those
of the author and do not necessarily reflect the views of the publisher,
and the publisher hereby disclaims any responsibility for them.

Any people depicted in stock imagery provided by Getty Images are models,
and such images are being used for illustrative purposes only.
Certain stock imagery © Getty Images.

Scripture quotations taken from the Revised English
Bible, copyright © Cambridge University Press and
Oxford University Press 1989. All rights reserved.

ISBN: 979-8-3850-0790-5 (sc)
ISBN: 979-8-3850-0791-2 (e)

Library of Congress Control Number: 2023917642

Print information available on the last page.

WestBow Press rev. date: 09/19/2023

But should you from there seek the Lord your God,
you will find him,
if it is with all your heart and soul that you search.
(Deuteronomy 4:29)

CONTENTS

What is Christianity?.. 1

The way, the truth and the life 6

God's chosen people 11

The Ten Commandments... 16

The new teaching.. 22

Living with others 27

True to the Faith or open to God?............................... 31

Holy week and on 36

Creative Spirit, Holy Spirit... 41

Jesus lifted up.. 45

The shepherd and the Gardener................................... 48

A good life 52

CONTENTS

1
2
11
16
27
31

WHAT IS CHRISTIANITY?

CHRISTIANITY COMES FROM THE TEACHING OF JESUS Christ. He lived at the beginning of the first century of the christian era, in what is now Israel. He was born in Bethlehem, in the then southern kingdom of Judah. He was brought up in the northern kingdom of Israel. That is where he began teaching.

Christians believe that in the beginning God made the world, and it was a good and happy place. Then early man ate fruit from the forbidden tree of the knowledge of good and evil. Ever since there has been a conflict between good and evil, evil giving problems and spoiling the good. Jesus gave us victory over evil, bringing back the life that God intended for us.

The Bible tells about Jesus in the four Gospels which begin the New Testament. The word *Gospel* is a corruption of the old english for *God's Word*. Each gospel writer wrote according to what he knew and what seemed important to him. St Luke began his Gospel with a statement that he had carefully researched his material.

> Many writers have undertaken to draw up an
> account of the events that have taken place

> among us, following the traditions handed
> down to us by the original eyewitnesses and
> servants of the gospel. So I in my turn, as one
> who has investigated the whole course of
> these events in detail, have decided to write
> an orderly narrative ... authentic knowledge
> about the matters of which you have been
> informed.
>
> (Luke 1:1–4)

The Old Testament is about the jewish people. It is the basis of judaism, from which Jesus drew his teaching. Judaism had rules set by God; people pleased God by keeping them. Jesus gave a new understanding of the rules. He turned religion into a way of living, the life for which God designed us.

Very few people want to be bad. But we all grow up with ideas we get from those around us, and so we get a mix of evil and good components. Thus we easily slip into keeping conventions and following the crowd. God has a better way for us.

In this world we find ourselves influenced and controlled by things of which we are not really fully aware. The wisdom of Jesus moves us away from that, into being a people of God.

The destructive influence in the world is God's enemy, Satan.

Jesus told a parable, to illustrate how God planted the world with good people, and Satan mixed in bad.

> A man sowed his field with good seed; but
> while everyone was asleep his enemy came,
> sowed darnel among the wheat, and made

> off. When the corn sprouted and began to
> fill out, the darnel could be seen among it. ...
> I will tell the reapers, 'Gather the darnel first,
> and tie it in bundles for burning; then collect
> the wheat into my barn.'
> (Matthew 13:24–30)

That was a trick which was sometimes done to get the better of someone. Darnel looks like wheat until the ears begin to form. The field was the world. The wheat was the people who had learned from God. The darnel looked the same. The enemy was Satan, who planted people with wrong ideas.

The parable explains that God let those people remain, so as not to accidently uproot any of the others. God gave them an opportunity to change.

Jesus taught us to recognise Satan's work for what it is and turn from it. By aligning ourselves with God we tap into God's power and guidance; God's wisdom surpasses all other. Thus our new life is easier and better. Quarrelling and squabbling are replaced by helping each other along and enjoying each other. Fears and worries disappear. We feel secure. We feel fulfilled.

Christianity brings back a quality of living that Satan took away. It is called the Kingdom of God.

A lot of people are half way there. Going the other half makes all the difference. Jesus' teaching releases the good which God built into people. It alerts us to mistakes that are easily made. Life gets better and better the further we get in. Christians work for God's Kingdom to take over the world.

Once, when Jesus made a move to continue his journey, the crowd pressed him not to leave them. They wanted him to stay and tell them more.

> But he said, 'I must give the good news of the
> kingdom of God to the other towns also, for
> that is what I was sent to do.'
> (Luke 4:43)

Preachers give various reasons, why Jesus came to Earth. Jesus himself said that he had come to give the good news of the Kingdom of God. That was his job description, from his own mouth.

We get a glimpse of God's Kingdom wherever people are living well and happily together. When we all get there, the world will be back to what God designed.

Some christians see Jesus as rescuing us from Satan's clutches. Some christians see Earth as a battlefield between God and Satan, with christians involved in spiritual warfare, fighting for God.

Jesus foresaw Satan's power increasing, and with it confusion and suffering on a big scale. Then the time will be ripe for Jesus to come again, the second coming.

> Jesus began: 'Be on your guard; let no one
> mislead you. Many will come claiming my
> name, and saying, "I am he"; and many will
> be misled by them. When you hear of wars
> and rumours of wars, do not be alarmed.
> Such things are bound to happen; but the
> end is still to come. For nation will go to war
> against nation, kingdom against kingdom;

> there will be earthquakes in many places;
> there will be famines. These are the first
> birth-pangs of the new age.
> (Mark 13:5–8, also Matthew chapter 24)

The new age is what, deep in our hearts, we long for—God's Kingdom established on Earth.

At the second coming Jesus will separate people into two groups. Satan and his followers will be taken away. Jesus himself will rule.

> Then the king will say to those on his right,
> "You have my Father's blessing; come, take
> possession of the kingdom that has been
> ready for you since the world was made.
> (Matthew 25:34)

Critics may see christianity as comfort for the feebleminded, or just not attainable. The discerning realise that it is a splendid thing to be what we should be.

THE WAY, THE TRUTH
AND THE LIFE

JESUS SAID THAT HE IS THE WAY, THE TRUE WAY, THAT brings us fullness of life.

> Jesus replied, 'I am the way, the truth, and the life; no one comes to the Father except by me.
> (John 14:6)

That is one of the 'I am' statements of Jesus, in which he used an analogy to explain himself. Christianity is sometimes referred to as 'the way'. Jesus described his teaching as 'the truth' and Satan's ideas as 'the lie'. By 'life' Jesus meant abundant life, more than just existing.

One we accept this, we can look into what Jesus said, to follow it. So begins the christian life. Jesus made it clear that we have to accept him and do as he taught. Until then we are playing with christianity and playing with God and playing with our own life.

As we go along in the christian life we discover more about Jesus. We do not have to decide straight away whether the miracles were real or whether he rose from the dead, and other things which seem impossible.

Jesus' aim was to show us God. When we know God his superior understanding safeguards us. A big gap has grown between man and God; Jesus is the bridge that spans it.

> If you knew me you would know my Father
> too ... Anyone who has seen me has seen the
> Father ... Do you not believe that I am in the
> Father, and the Father in me?
> (John 14:7–10)

That relationship is fundamental. We look up to God. Christians speak of dwelling in God and God dwelling in us. When we know God really well then his goodness flows into us and on through us into our world. That is how our world benefits from the christians in it. People should recognise that, and be grateful to us.

When we all have that relationship we all live our lives aright and the world comes right. The world's problems gradually vanish. King Charles III of the United Kingdom and Commonwealth said just that in his coronation service. He promised to bring his realms to that standing with God. That was his plan to remove his people's problems.

Jesus spoke of God as his Father. He meant a loving relationship, like that of a parent. We must not forget that God created us, as well as everything else. God and his children make up the great christian family. It is in every part of the world.

Jesus not only taught us about God, his teaching was from God.

> I am not myself the source of the words I
> speak to you: it is the Father who dwells in
> me doing his own work.
> (John 14: 10)

We imagine that Jesus picked up the scriptures as a boy, from attending synagogue each sabbath with Mary, his mother, and Joseph, his stepfather. They also went to festivals in Jerusalem. Once, when he was twelve years old, he got left behind. Mary and Joseph had to go back to look for him.

> ...and after three days they found him
> sitting in the temple surrounded by the
> teachers, listening to them and putting
> questions; and all who heard him were
> amazed at his intelligence and the answers
> he gave.
> (Luke 2:46–47)

Those days with the leading religious experts of the country sharpened Jesus' knowledge of jewish belief. At the same time Jesus formulated a more profound understanding of the scriptures than they had. But Mary was worried and reprimanded him.

> 'Why did you search for me?' he said. 'Did
> you not know that I was bound to be in my
> Father's house?'
> (Luke 2:49)

Some readings give '...about my Father's business'.

Throughout his ministry Jesus taught in synagogues and in the temple. Jesus gained a crowd of followers, whom he also taught. Jesus went out to all classes of his community.

St Matthew's Gospel gives the fullest account we have of Jesus' teaching. St John's Gospel keeps veering off the story onto who Jesus was; he was God's Son, sent to put the world right. We need to put the four Gospels together carefully, to get a full picture of Jesus.

As his following increased, the religious leaders began to watch carefully what he was saying.

Jesus always pointed people away from themselves. He pointed them away from worrying to trusting God. Trust in God was to remove the element of doubt, fear and insecurity from our lives.

> Set your troubled hearts at rest. Trust in God
> always; trust also in me.
> (John 14:1)

Having complete peace of mind at all moments is a vital gift which Jesus' teaching gives us.

> If you stand by my teaching, you are truly
> my disciples; you will know the truth, and
> the truth will set you free.
> (John 8:31–32)

Jesus cut across fancy ideas and mistaken beliefs to bring people to see truly what life was about. He saw mankind bound by needless chains: fears and apprehensions, social demands, ambition, greed—and many more, which we can easily name. Jesus saw them as unnecessary, if only we arrange our lives aright. He came to show us how.

If we think about it, surely that is true.

GOD'S CHOSEN PEOPLE

THE BIBLE GIVES A GENEALOGY OF THE DESCENDANTS OF the couple who ate fruit from the forbidden tree. It traces their progeny to Abram, who was living in Ur of the Chaldees, the first great human civilisation, now Iraq.

> The Lord said to Abram, 'Leave your own country, your kin, and your father's house, and go to a country that I will show you. I shall make you into a great nation; I shall bless you and make your name so great that it will be used in blessings:
>
> those who bless you, I shall bless;
> those who curse you, I shall curse.
> All the peoples on earth
> will wish to be blessed as you are blessed.
> (Genesis 12:1–3)

Abram's descendants are the jews and from this text he is the patriarch of the jewish nation; they are God's chosen people. When we look today at the achievements of jews in finance, the arts and science, God's blessing rings true.

Abram completed the journey in two stages, arriving at the Oak Trees of Mamre, now Transjordan. There God made a covenant with him, that is, a solemn, binding agreement. It extended to Abram's descendants. God was to be their God and they were to be his people. All the land around was to be theirs. The name Abram meant High Father. God changed it to Abraham, which means Father of Many. God was to be the High Father of his people.

The Bible continues the family history. However, as generations went by, the people kept losing sight of God and of the covenant. Thus they missed out on having God as their Father and on the blessing.

After a time famine caused them to go to Egypt. Only when their life there deteriorated did they want to go back. God gave them a leader, Moses. On the way they paused at Mount Sinai. God, speaking through Moses, gave them rules to keep them together and on track with him. They were the Ten Commandments and the Law of Moses.

Meanwhile the promised land had been occupied by another people, giants. Instead of turning to God they were intimidated and went no further. A whole generation passed and their wanderings brought them to the other side of the land. Then, with a new leader, Joshua, they asked God how to proceed. They had to conquer a walled city. God gave them a curious strategy, and it worked (Joshua 6:1–20).

They settled in the land as a loose confederation of the twelve tribes; the twelve original families had grown into tribes. They had the Law. Judges settled disputes. God was their leader, protector and guide. That was the way God had for people to live.

But the next generation of judges went astray. The people turned to wanting a king. God let them have their way. It did not work out well.

God appointed the second king, David, through a prophet. David brought the kingdom together. He set up Jerusalem as the capital. He built the royal palace. He collected the best quality materials to build a magnificent temple for God in the highest part of the city, overlooking the Mount of Olives. His son, Solomon, organised its building. In Jesus' day that period was thought of as the good old days of their greatness. They longed to have them back.

The good days did not last long. Babylon invaded. The temple was looted. The people were deported. God brought one good thing from it. Babylon was a higher civilisation. It had writing. The scholarly among the jews put the scriptures, which had been handed down orally, into a written record.

Years later a remnant went back to rebuild Jerusalem. With the routine of everyday life, the relationship with God again slackened. There were ups and downs. Eventually the promised land was absorbed into the Roman Empire.

Studies from the ancient scriptures led the jews to expect a Messiah to come and bring the old days back. Jesus was not the kind of Messiah they expected. He had God's thinking, not theirs. He brought a new and different concept of kingdom, the Kingdom of God. It was something much bigger. It was not political. It cut across political boundaries. We were all to be part of it, if we would.

Bringing christians to be God's chosen people did not take God away from the jews. The plan is for the whole world. Jesus said to his disciples:

> I have called you friends, because I have
> disclosed to you everything that I heard
> from my Father. You did not choose me: I
> chose you. I appointed you to go on and bear
> fruit, fruit that will last; so that the Father
> may give you whatever you ask in my name.
> (John 15:15–16)

The fruit is partly the way we develop and perfect our life, to become a truly godly person. Added to that is for communities and countries to live happily together. Everyone should know Jesus' way, understand it and do it. Then all are God's chosen people, the world is his Kingdom, blessed by him. We can see this as the world back on track.

God had created an evolving world. In some directions evolution has gone ahead nicely. Human life has improved. In other directions life has got more and more unsatisfactory. The pace is getting faster and faster, in both the good and the wrong direction.

We had the renaissance, bringing a new dimension of knowledge, with the arts and science, into our lives. Then the industrial revolution, and now the technological revolution. We have arrived at exciting hopes of uncovering more and more knowledge, as God leads us along. We think of our understanding of how the world was made coming to conquer illness and aging and we know not what more. Our world is also in tumult and confusion.

The building blocks of modern chemistry, physics and electronics were there in the creation, in the atomic structure of matter, ready to be used when the time came. Such is God's far reaching mind. We do not know what else lies waiting for us, out of God's creation. Those are humble and hopeful thoughts with which to fill our minds.

We christians are the people God has chosen to make his world. Just now we need to shake ourselves, to get out of being bogged down in narrow, limited thinking, and become worthy of the God who made us and fit for the world he made for us.

THE TEN COMMANDMENTS

1 You must have no other gods beside me.

2 You are not to make a carved image for yourself ...
   You must not worship or serve them.

3 You shall not make wrong use of the name of the
   Lord your God; the Lord will not leave unpunished
   anyone who misuses his name.

4 Observe the sabbath day and keep it holy as the
   Lord your God commanded you. You have six days
   to labour and do all your work; but the seventh day
   there is a sabbath of the Lord your God; that day
   you must not do any work, neither you, nor your son
   or your daughter ... your ox, your donkey, or any of
   your cattle, or the alien residing among you, so that
   your slaves and slave-girls may rest as you do.

5 Honour your father and your mother, as the Lord
   your God commanded you, so that you may enjoy
   long life, and it will be well with you in the land which
   the Lord your God is giving you.

6 Do not commit murder.

7 Do not commit adultery.

8 Do not steal.

9 Do not give baseless evidence against your neighbour.

10 Do not lust after your neighbour's wife; do not covet
your neighbour's household, his land … his ox, his
donkey, or anything that belongs to him.
(Deuteronomy 5:7–21)

GOD GAVE THE TEN COMMANDMENTS AND THE LAW TO
the jews while they were travelling back to the promised land
from Egypt. As they were given by God, we expect them to
be correct and not need modification. Jesus said that he had
not come to change the Law, but to fill it out more completely.
Thus the Ten Commandments are the basic code of conduct
for our lives today.

> Do not suppose that I have come to abolish
> the law and the prophets; I did not come to
> abolish, but to complete. Truly I tell you: so
> long as heaven and earth endure, not a letter,
> not a dot, will disappear from the law until
> all that must happen has happened.
> (Matthew 5:18)

An alternative reading for the last words is *before all that
it stands for is achieved.* When God's Kingdom comes in its
fullness, then laws will no longer be needed; people will do
naturally what the law requires.

Today countries draw up a considerably more extensive
sets of laws. They allow for all the many ways in which a
person can go wrong with Satan at large. Legal experts
interpret them and pronounce over details. Ordinary people
carry a general idea of their country's laws in their head and
conduct themselves according to that, without knowing all
the details. That is enough get along with.

The jews of old added details to the commandments, to make them more specific to apply. The basics became obscured by the overlay.

God conceived the commandments in a totally different way. They were not rules that had to be obeyed but an indication of satisfactory behaviour. God knows how we are. The Law stood to keep people together, by avoiding situations which disrupt our relation with God and with each other.

Jesus' teaching went back to that purpose. He completed the Law by enlarging on some of the points, and so giving them greater meaning. We should understand the Commandments in the light of the explanations that Jesus gave.

The commandments start with our relationship with God. How we relate to God oversees the rest. The first three commandments address slackness towards God; forgetting God had kept holding the jews back.

In ancient times, people carved images and used them as gods. Not knowing God, it gave them something outside themselves to which to refer. People might carry a charm for good luck. The first commandments tell us to be serious about God, nothing of superstition or magic.

Some christians today wear a cross. It is not a charm. It discretely tells people that they are a christian. It tells other christians that they are one of them.

The fourth commandment appoints a rest day, the sabbath. Everyone needs a rest day, those who work for us and working animals too. When God created the world he worked for six days, then on the seventh day he rested. The sabbath also celebrates the creation.

This commandment is spelled out in some detail. Perhaps that encouraged the jews to hold closely to it, which they did.

They labelled some things as permitted on the sabbath and others as work. A strict jew today will not displease God by switching on an electric light on the sabbath. That was work, as was healing. Their commitment, but not the belief, puts christians to shame.

The fifth commandment is greatly neglected today. It calls on children and adults to respect their parents. It links long life and well being with honouring one's parents. To have a long and happy life in the land the Lord has given us to live, we honour our parents, and look after them in need, and parents make themselves worthy of honour.

The remaining commandments tell us not to do silly things, which will obviously upset our neighbours. If we do them, that eats into our own life too.

The modern world has produced modern situations and modern sins, which Jesus' day did not know.

Modern advertising does not tell us what the thing does, so that we can decide whether it will be useful to us or not. Carefully chosen words and images, backed by psychology, seek to make us want it, even if we do not have a use for it, or if there may be another one which is better for us. Our planet's resources are frittered away, making it all.

Internet provides us with instant access to each other and to information, broadcasting and much more. God gave some people insight and ability to bring it about. Satan got into some such people to abuse their skill, and to abuse God, by hacking into computers, indoctrinating people, trapping young people into drugs or pornography, or people trafficking.

Society needs to remove these people. Converting them is positive. Putting them away in prisons for years admits that society has failed.

There are national leaders who use their power for personal gain, or just flounder along. Some set themselves up to force their ethics on others. They do not ask what reasons the others have for doing things differently.

Jesus broadened the commandments. He extended murder to killing a person's character, and adultery to looking at a woman lustfully (Matthew 5:21 and 5:27).

In essence, Jesus replaced bald instructions by principles. It was the spirit of the Law that was to be on our hearts and always in our minds.

> For this is the covenant I shall establish with the Israelites ... I shall set my law within them, writing it on their hearts; I shall be their God, and they will be my people. No longer need they teach one another, neighbour or brother, to know the Lord; all of them, high and low alike, will know me, says the Lord...
> (Jeremiah 31:33–34)

It is easy to think that Jesus' principles are out of date. Jesus is outside time. He knew the world at its beginning and at its end. The end is God's Kingdom. What Jesus taught led to that.

In all this teaching Jesus calls upon his people to look beyond appearances and beyond ourselves. We need God's perspective to guide us; he looks down on the world from above.

We look first to God, then to those around us. We set the other person's point of view alongside ours. We understand their position, their thinking, their feelings. Then we can balance theirs and ours, and both of us gain. Jesus put it in a simple way.

> Always treat others as you would like them
> to treat you: that is the law and the prophets.
> (Matthew 7:12)

THE NEW TEACHING

THE GOSPEL OF ST MATTHEW GIVES THE CORE OF JESUS'
teaching. He devoted three chapters to it, that is how
important he saw it to be. It is prefaced by the Beatitudes, or
blessings. People have puzzled over these, since they seem all
wrong. Jesus was drawing attention to the upside down world,
and what he was going to do to it.

> Blessed are the poor in spirit;
> the kingdom of Heaven is theirs.
> Blessed are the sorrowful;
> they shall find consolation.
> Blessed are the gentle;
> they shall have the earth for their possession.
> Blessed are those who hunger and thirst to
> see right prevail;
> they shall be satisfied.
> Blessed are those who show mercy;
> mercy shall be shown to them.
> Blessed are those whose hearts are pure;
> they shall see God.
> Blessed are the peacemakers;
> they shall be called God's children.

Blessed are those who are persecuted in the
cause of right;
the kingdom of Heaven is theirs.
(Matthew 5:3–10)

The Kingdom of Heaven is Matthew's phrase for the Kingdom of God.

From the Beatitudes we can pick out a list of christian attributes: sorrow for wrong things, gentleness, right should prevail, mercy, purity, keeping the peace.

These attributes do not make us a christian. Holding them shows that we identify with (some of) God's wishes for the world. Jesus did not ask us to seek the attributes. That would make us an actor, dressed up to look the part. Jesus wanted his listeners to come to see how God had in mind for the world to be. Then we can adjust ourselves to that end.

There are parts of Jesus' teaching with which we can easily agree. The deeper bits require some effort. We have to rethink our own attitudes. That is more demanding. There is a natural tendency to skip those bits. If we do we discard the most valuable part of all and fail to achieve the objective.

Jesus put forward a new commandment, as he called it. It was his great commandment of love.

I give you a new commandment: love one
another; as I have loved you, so you are to
love one another. If there is this love among
you, then everyone will know that you are
my disciples.
(John 13:34–35)

23

Just as Jesus' love went to everyone, we are to love everyone, whoever they are. It is to be second nature to us. That is how we step over from worldly thinking to be with God. That is what it is to imitate Jesus. Then the Kingdom comes to us and we enter into the Kingdom.

The principle of loving our neighbour has an obvious liberating effect. Look at it from the position of the neighbour. To be treated lovingly by everyone removes barriers. It brings out the good in each one of us. Life takes on a new dimension. We are all born into the world together; we become God's Kingdom by the way we live together.

Jesus' new commandment was not, in fact, new. The Gospel of St Luke tells that a lawyer asked Jesus, 'Teacher, what must I do to inherit eternal life?' Jesus turned the question back on him; he was the expert who had studied the law, he was the one to have the answer.

> Jesus said, 'What is written in the law? What is your reading of it?' He replied, 'Love the Lord your God with all your heart, and with all your soul, with all your strength, and with all your mind; and your neighbour as yourself.' 'That is the right answer,' said Jesus; 'do that and you will have life.'
> (Luke 10:26–28)

The lawyer gave the answer from the ancient book of the Law (Deuteronomy 6:4–5): first love God, then love your neighbour. Jesus said to him, in effect, 'You know it, do it'. That is where the difficulty comes. Loving God and our neighbour with our all touches on so much. We do not take it nearly far enough. It needs working over and over. What Matthew wrote is only a pointer from which to start.

Jesus extended the principle of love in a startling way.

> But what I tell you is this: Love your enemies
> and pray for your persecutors; only so can
> you be children of your heavenly Father...
> (Matthew 5:44–45)

Loving a hostile or unpleasant person is where it is natural to draw the line. Jesus said that instead of feeling a rebuff we should think that that person has failed to love as they should; they have the problem, not us. We may not know what has made them how they are, but they need our help to get out of it.

That is how we should see other people's faults. Lack of consideration and bad behaviour are cries for help. That is how God sees it. If we do not, we are not with God. Helping each other along, going out of our way to do it, is fundamental in the new teaching.

A further revolutionary teaching of Jesus is 'turn the other cheek', that is, if someone molests one, do not fight back.

> Do not resist those who wrong you. If anyone
> slaps you on the right cheek, turn and offer
> him the other also.
> (Matthew 5:39)

Defending ourself continues the aggression. A little thing becomes something bigger. It takes two to have a quarrel.

Hitting back repeats the other's wrong action. Turning the other cheek is a simple rebuke. We should leave God to settle such issues, not take it into our own hands. He knows what was behind it all. He can discipline the one who started it, better than we can.

Jesus went on to say that if someone takes your shirt on pledge, let him have your cloak as well. If someone in authority presses you into service for one mile, as roman soldiers did, go with him two.

Jesus' principle was to preserve peace. Put that before insisting on one's rights. Instead, return wrong with good. Leave God to recompense us.

Jesus added, 'Give to anyone who asks, do not turn your back on a borrower' (Matthew 5:39–42).

Satan would have us drawn into doing doubtful things. Jesus said, 'No'. As his followers we pursue the way of peace. God gives a just settlement.

Jesus referred to adopting the new teaching as being 'born again'.

> Jesus answered, 'In very truth I tell you, no
> one can see the kingdom of God unless he
> has been born again.'
> (John 3:3)

He spoke of being born of water and the Spirit. Water refers to river baptism. It simulates drowning. It symbolises dying to the world's ways. Then one is born again by the Holy Spirit into God's ways.

LIVING WITH OTHERS

THE LAWYER IN THE PREVIOUS SECTION PUSHED HIS question further. He asked, 'Who is my neighbour?' Jesus answered him with the parable of the Good Samaritan.

The parable tells of a man who fell among thieves. They robbed him and left him for dead. Two passers by were too busy to stop, or did not notice. It could easily happen today. The samaritan saw and stopped. He put the man on his donkey, took him to an inn and left him in the care of the inn keeper. He left some money. He promised to come back. He promised to pay any more that may be needed.

The parable did not answer the lawyer's question. Instead it indicated the fullness that our love should have. We are left to think that our neighbour is anyone in need. In fact our neighbour is everyone with whom we come into contact.

The parable is interesting, since it introduces a new christian concept, compassion.

The Good Samaritan shows us the nature of loving, as opposed to sympathy or kindness. It is the kind of love expressed by the greek word *agape*. That is the very deepest of the four words greek had for love. It is a very deep and complete love.

Today most people would stop and help a person in trouble. The question Jesus raises is, would we do as much as the samaritan did, and him a foreigner. Jesus pointed to how God would have all our relationships to be, including casual ones or chance contacts.

Jesus went further. He told us to love our enemies. In the Kingdom of God there are no enemies. In the world there is one enemy, Satan. He is God's enemy and ours. Those who oppose us or treat us badly or roughly have been taken over by him. They are not enemies. They are simply being used. They are people to love and rescue.

Jesus taught never to condemn a person, but always to forgive them, whatever the case may be. God shows mercy. 'Blessed are those who show mercy; mercy shall be shown to them'.

Along with that Jesus told us not to judge people.

> Do not judge, and you will not be judged. For
> as you judge others, so you will yourselves be
> judged, and whatever measure you deal out
> to others will be dealt to you.
> (Matthew 7:1–2)

That is very true; we get back what we give.

If we judge a person we do not know what made them like that. It may not be their fault that we have advanced further in the Lord's way than they have. We may have a fault that we have not noticed.

> Why do you look at the speck in your
> brother's eye, with never a thought for the
> plank in your own? ... You hypocrite! First

> take the plank out of your own eye, and then
> you will see clearly to take the speck out of
> your brother's.
> (Luke 6:41–42)

So we look at people lovingly, without an inflated opinion of ourself. We bear with their failings. The worst thing is to criticise a person behind their back. If we feel strongly about something they do, then confess our feeling to them. Do it privately. Read Matthew 18:15–17.

We should not wrong other people, and if we do we can ask them to forgive us. Throughout his teaching Jesus attached importance to forgiveness. It brings healing to a damaged relationship, to both sides. Forgiving a person is a way of loving and helping them.

Whenever we say the Lord's Prayer, whether in church or in our prayers at home or whenever, we tell God that we have forgiven those who have offended us; we ask God to forgive us in the same way that we have forgiven.

> And forgive us our sins,
> for we too forgive all who have done us
> wrong.
> (Luke 11:4)

The disciple, Peter, asked Jesus how often he should forgive his brother if he went on wronging him and apologising (Matthew 18:21). Peter suggested as many as seven times. Seven was considered to be the perfect number. Peter surely thought that that was exercising great restraint. Jesus replied, in effect, 'No. No. Seventy times seven'. No one would count four hundred and ninety times. What was Jesus saying?

We can think of Christianity as a religion of new beginnings—for us when we go wrong, for anyone who makes a mistake. Forgive and forget. Make a new start, with the experience of what happened behind one. Next time we can do things better. Surely that is better than harbouring grievance. That is not what Satan has taught the world. Forgiveness is a born again attitude.

Jesus' new thinking converts us to God's thinking. God does not see friends and enemies, he sees people who have picked up worldly ways and his ways, a mixture, some more one way, some more the other. Each generation makes adjustments. After two thousand years, loving Jesus' way is still a neglected christian practice. Mankind could have been there all that time ago, if only enough people had made an effort to understand Jesus.

TRUE TO THE FAITH
OR OPEN TO GOD?

JESUS COMING TO EARTH WAS A DECLARATION OF WAR ON Satan. Satan fought back. He still fights back. Jesus said:

> You must not think that I have come to bring
> peace to the earth; I have not come to bring
> peace, but a sword. I have come to set a man
> against his mother ... a man will find his
> enemies under his own roof.
> (Matthew 10:34-36)

The new teaching touched people in different ways. Quite a lot saw sense in it. Some saw God in Jesus and behind him because he did miracles of healing; only God could do such a thing.

But Jesus' teaching was radical. Moreover he did things that labelled him as not respecting God. He healed on the sabbath; healing was considered to be work and a violation of God's commandment to keep the sabbath holy. He was accused of blasphemy; blasphemy is putting oneself equal to God. He hobnobbed with disreputable people.

> Jesus answered them: 'It is not the healthy
> that need a doctor, but the sick; I have not
> come to call the virtuous but sinners to
> repentance.'
> (Luke 5:31–32)

Jesus was clear in his own mind. That annoyed the
leaders, who stuck to their position, even when they could not
defend it against his. That happened especially over healing
on the sabbath.

> Then he turned to them: 'Is it permitted to
> do good or to do evil on the sabbath, to save
> life or to kill?' They had nothing to say...
> (Mark 3:4)

Jesus waited for an answer. Silence. Then he did the
miracle. There was a mixed reaction. The healed person
praised God. The religious people plotted how to remove
Jesus.

Jesus insisted that the sabbath rule was not made to
please God but to benefit man.

> The sabbath was made for man, not man for
> the sabbath: so the Son of Man is lord even
> of the sabbath.
> (Mark 2:27–28)

Jesus asserted his supreme authority, which was from
God. He opened up the observance of the sabbath from being
a list of things to do and not do. He brought in principles of
right and wrong. The sabbath was to be a benefit to man. We

should observe the sabbath in that spirit, either on saturday or sunday, as is the custom in our locality.

The wealthy and powerful made up five percent of the population. Mary and Joseph were in the lowest class; a carpenter was not a skilled craftsman, he was a person who had lost his land and had to work for his living. Jesus did not go down well with some of the powerful. They were used to telling people, not being advised or challenged. Leaders tend to be like that today.

The Jewish Council, lead by the High Priest, managed jewish affairs. They were under the roman governor. Scribes were professionals who advised on the law and saw to it being kept. Pharisees were a political party which stood by the letter of the Law.

Religion centred on the temple. Not so long afterwards the temple was destroyed. It had to be. It was corrupt. People gave an animal or a bird to atone for each sin they had committed, like paying a fine. The priests sacrificed them at the altar. The altar was a place of sacrifice, not of worship.

Jesus called for people to turn from sin to God. A good number of the upper class saw sense in what Jesus said. But the top leaders kept a tight grip on the reigns.

That was not what Jesus wished. Jesus wanted reform, not to split judaism. However, the guardians of judaism forced the birth of christianity.

Certainly Jesus did not come to bring peace but a sword, as he does today. Good meaning people get Jesus wrong, or get just a part of his message. Today's church has denominations, who rarely come together. Satan has removed its influence.

What is clear today is the extent to which wrong living has entered the world. It was not new in Jesus' day. The prophets of old had pointed out dishonest tricks, bad practices, self-centredness, dishonesty and insincerity.

> For crime after crime of Israel
> I shall grant them no reprieve,
> because they sell honest folk for silver
> and the poor for a pair of sandals.
> They grind the heads of the helpless into the dust
> and push the humble out of their way.
> Father and son resort to the temple girls,
> so profaning my holy name.
> Men lie down beside every altar
> on garments held in pledge,
> and in the house of their God they drink wine
> on the proceeds of fines.
> (Amos 2:6–8)

Those words ring bells in our ears today. 'No reprieve' is hard. Teaching a worthy life style nailed Jesus to the cross.

Still today there are people who hold that, to get on in the world, one has to do as the world does. Then one gets money. Then one can buy anything one wants. St Paul advised the danger of overrating money and making it a god.

> The love of money is the root of all evil, and
> in pursuit of it some have wandered from
> the faith and spiked themselves on many a
> painful thorn.
> (1 Timothy 6:10)

Jesus turned attention onto a way of living that was not centred on things but on people. We were designed to be gregarious. Jesus did not teach prosperity, but godliness and the common good.

It should be easier for us today. God has made people who invent appliances which make the daily tasks easy and others who set up social services. Those bring a further gift, leisure time. We should use it well. But our minds are on secondary or tertiary things. We mention primary things, but act little on them.

St John's Gospel opens with calling Jesus *the Word*. Jesus came from God, God's Word to give light to man.

> In the beginning the Word already was. The Word was in God's presence, and what God was, the Word was. He was with God at the beginning, and through him all things came to be; without him no created thing came into being. In him was life, and that life was the light of mankind. The light shines in the darkness, and the darkness has never mastered it.
> (John 1:1–5)

Jesus is a light shining in a dark world. Light always conquers darkness, if we do our part and let it.

HOLY WEEK AND ON

HOLY WEEK MARKS THE CLIMAX OF JESUS' TIME ON EARTH. It begins with the triumphal entry into Jerusalem; the crowds spread palm branches and their clothes on the ground to carpet his way, and hailed him king. A roman triumph was the majestic reception home of a general who had won a great victory.

The happenings of holy week were far from holy. Jesus had never trusted the crowds. He once told his disciples that they listened and listened, but did not understand (Mark 4:10–12). They wanted to crown him king and drive the romans out.

The crowd was fickle. In the space of a few days their cry changed from 'Hosanna', a cry of praise, to 'Crucify him'. It was to be the cruel roman execution by torture, suspended by the arms, tied, outstretched, to a cross. In this case, the hands were nailed.

Knowing full well what was to be, Jesus went to Jerusalem for the jewish festival.

Jesus taught openly in the temple. A great power came over him. No one dared touch him. He gave his final teaching to the Twelve, preparing them to take over from him. There came the Last Supper, the betrayal and the arrest.

The Bible (John 13:21–30) records an interesting private conversation during the supper. Then Jesus discretely sent Judas out to betray him.

> Jesus said to him, 'Do quickly what you have
> to do.' No one at the table understood what
> he meant by this.
> (John 13:27–28)

After supper, Jesus took his disciples to a quiet place outside the city to pray. It was late.

Jesus was overwhelmed with grief (Matthew 26:36–39). It was not for himself, it was for what the rulers and the people were throwing away.

Then came the arrest. One of Jesus' followers drew a sword. He cut off the high priest's servant's ear. Jesus did his last miracle. He put the ear back. The servant was only a servant, obeying orders.

The trial was a battle of wills. The high priest and his aides wanted the death sentence. Only the roman governor, Pontius Pilate, had authority to give it. The charge was stirring up the crowds to rebellion. Pilate's wife intervened on behalf of Jesus.

Jesus declined to answer questions. Pilate reminded him that he had power to release or crucify him. In that desperate situation Jesus asserted God's control. He told Pilate that he would have no power over him unless it were given from above. He added that those who accused him were more guilty than Pilate. Read the whole story in the Gospel of St John, chapter 18.

From that point Pilate tried hard to release Jesus. Several times he gave a 'not guilty' verdict. But the religious leaders would not have it.

Jesus referred to his Kingdom. Pilate asked him if he was a king.

> Jesus answered, '"King" is your word. My
> task is to bear witness to the truth. For this
> I was born; for this I came into the world,
> and all who are not deaf to truth listen to
> my voice.'
> (John 18:37)

The roman soldiers put a purple robe on Jesus and pressed a crown of thorns onto his head.

Pilate had Jesus scourged. A scourge was a short whip of nine thongs. They had metal ends, sharpened to cut the skin. The back was given fifty flicks, less one.

The religious leaders whipped up the crowd to the point of civil disorder.

> When Pilate saw that he was getting
> nowhere, and that there was danger of a riot,
> he took water and washed his hands in full
> view of the crowd. 'My hands are clean of
> this man's blood,' he declared. 'See to that
> yourselves.' With one voice the people cried,
> 'His blood be on us and on our children.'
> (Matthew 27:24–25)

How could anyone wish such a thing on their children! But it happens today; people repeat things without thinking. The Diaspora Museum in Tel Aviv is a documented record of jews scattered around the world and abused. The land of Israel today is smaller than the covenant gave. There is hostility between Israel and its neighbours.

After the trial even the roman soldiers joined in abusing Jesus (Matthew 27:27–30). Jesus went to the cross, thinking how it would rebound on everyone.

> Great numbers of people followed, among them many women who mourned and lamented over him. Jesus turned to them and said, 'Daughters of Jerusalem, do not weep for me; weep for yourselves and your children.'
> (Luke 23:27–28)

It is a sad story, of God's Kingdom thrown away, by God's chosen people. It has come to us. Horrible things happen, when Satan gets into people.

Naked on the cross, suspended by his arms, Jesus was offered a bitter drink. It would have deadened his pain nerves. It would have deadened the brain cells which felt the pain. Jesus refused it.

> Jesus said, 'Father, forgive them; they do not know what they are doing.'
> They shared out his clothes by casting lots. The people stood looking on, and their rulers jeered at him: 'He saved others: now let him save himself, if this is God's Messiah, his Chosen.' The soldiers joined in the mockery...
> (Luke 23:34–36)

The crucifixion was intended to be the end. The sabbath over, a couple of faithful women went early on the sunday morning to the tomb. It was open and empty. Two angels said to them, 'He has risen, as he said he would'.

Easter Day celebrates the resurrection.

The story continues in the Gospels and in the second part of St Luke's treatise, the Acts of the Apostles. The word *disciple* means *pupil*, as in a school. *Apostle* means *one who is sent*.

> In the first part of my work, Theophilus, I gave an account of all that Jesus did and taught from the beginning until the day when he was taken up to heaven, after giving instructions through the Holy Spirit to the apostles whom he had chosen. To these men he showed himself after his death and gave ample proof that he was alive: he was seen by them over a period of forty days and spoke to them about the kingdom of God. While he was in their company he directed them not to leave Jerusalem. 'You must wait', he said, 'for the gift promised by the Father, of which I told you...
> (Acts 1:1–4)

CREATIVE SPIRIT, HOLY SPIRIT

THE DISCIPLES, NOW APOSTLES, PRAYED AND CHOSE another to take the place of Judas and make up The Twelve. They waited in Jerusalem as instructed.

> The day of Pentecost had come, and they were all together in one place. Suddenly there came from the sky what sounded like a strong, driving wind, a noise which filled the whole house where they were sitting. And there appeared to them flames like tongues of fire distributed among them and coming to rest on each one. They were all filled with the Holy Spirit and began to talk in other tongues, as the Spirit gave them power of utterance.
> (Acts 2:1–4)

Jews from all over were in Jerusalem for the festival. Peter spoke to them. Miraculously, each one heard him as if he was speaking their language. Guided by the Spirit, he spoke straight. He finished by telling them to repent and be baptized, every one of them, in the name of Jesus the Messiah. A lot of them did it, three thousand devout jews.

Thus the Holy Spirit created the church. It was not only there, but all over the roman world, as the converted went back to their homes after the festival. The apostles had to wait in the right place for the right time for it to happen.

The Bible continues the story in the Acts of the Apostles, as the Holy Spirit led the apostles on.

The Holy Spirit was at work in the creation of our planet. The Holy Spirit gave it form and order.

> In the beginning God created the heavens
> and the earth. The earth was a vast waste,
> darkness covered the deep, and the spirit
> of God hovered over the surface of the
> water.
> (Genesis 1:1–2)

Around 1950 an Oxford scientist, Dr. Fred Hoyle, an atheist, was making a name for himself as a cosmologist. At his retirement he made a far reaching statement. His life's scientific studies had forced him to the conclusion that the evolution of the universe had been guided by an intelligence. His scientific argument was that there had not been enough time since the big bang for the universe to reach its present state by chance. He said that it was as if at each stage an intelligence had instructed 'this way, not that'. We see there the Holy Spirit guiding evolution.

When the time came for Jesus to be born, an angel spoke to Mary. An angel is a messenger from God. We can be God's angel, when he gives us a message to tell.

> Then the angel said to her, '...you will conceive
> and give birth to a son, and you are to give
> him the name Jesus... The Lord God will give
> him the throne of his ancestor David, and
> he will be king over Israel for ever; his reign
> shall never end... The Holy Spirit will come
> upon you, and the power of the Most High
> will overshadow you; for that reason the holy
> child to be born will be called Son of God.
> (Luke 1:30–35)

Mary was going to bear a son by the Holy Spirit. Jesus' father was God, his mother was Mary.

In due course Jesus went to John the Baptist to be baptised. John was baptising by immersion in the river Jordan. In some places churches baptise in rivers today.

> ...the heavens were opened and he saw the
> Spirit of God descending like a dove to alight
> on him. And there came a voice from heaven
> saying, 'This is my beloved Son, in whom I
> take delight.'
> (Matthew 3:16–17)

Through the ages God's Spirit has come to his people in various forms. To us he speaks as a little voice inside us. Sometimes it is a conviction that grows on us. It is important to learn to recognise the voice and equally important to act on it.

God seems as if he has three faces. In theological terminology, they are the three persons of the Trinity: Father,

Son, Holy Spirit. We have the teaching of Jesus, the voice of
the Holy Spirit, and behind both is God.

The Holy Spirit was Jesus' parting gift to us. He gave it
with a condition.

> If you love me you will obey my commands;
> and I will ask the Father, and he will give
> you another to be your advocate, who will be
> with you for ever– the Spirit of truth.
> (John 14:15–17)

Jesus called the Holy Spirit *the Spirit of Truth*. In Jesus'
teaching God's truth opposes Satan's lie.

> However, when the Spirit of truth comes,
> he will guide you into all the truth; for he
> will not speak on his own authority, but will
> speak only what he hears...
> (John 16:13)

The Holy Spirit speaks from God. In moments of doubt
or choice he creates in us a certainty, what to do, where to
go, what to say. It may be to answer a question that is on our
mind. The Spirit answers our uncertainty.

Faith is not hoping, it is living by the Spirit. The Holy
Spirit does not solve our problems for us. He creates for us a
new kind of life without problems. Problems come when we
do no hear God's Spirit.

JESUS LIFTED UP

1 Just as Moses lifted up the serpent in the wilderness, so the Son of Man must be lifted up, in order that everyone who has faith may in him have eternal life.

2 God so loved the world that he gave his only Son, that everyone who has faith in him may not perish but have eternal life.

3 It was not to judge the world that God sent his Son into the world, but that through him the world might be saved.

4 No one who puts his faith in him comes under judgement; but the unbeliever has already been judged because he has not put his trust in God's only Son. This is the judgement: the light has come into the world, but people preferred darkness to light because their deeds were evil.

5 Wrongdoers hate the light and avoid it, for fear their misdeeds should be exposed. Those who live by the truth come to the light so that it may be clearly seen that God is in all they do.
(John 3:14–21)

AFTER THE CRUCIFIXION THE JEWISH LEADERS FELT success. They had put Jesus out of the way, as they thought, and preserved judaism. In fact they had caused christianity to emerge as a new faith, superseding theirs. Today Jesus lives in millions of believers all over the world, including Israel.

The passage quoted gives a sequence of five explanations, commenting on Jesus' intervention in the world. Each follows on from the previous one.

The first one draws on an incident when Moses was leading the jews from Egypt back to the promised land. They encountered venomous snakes. Some of the people were bitten and died. Moses had a bronze snake made and set up on a pole. Anyone bitten who looked at it and believed survived the bite. The story is in Numbers 21:6–29.

The text states that, in the same way, anyone who looks in faith to Jesus lifted up on the cross has eternal life: eternal life is the true life, the quality of which never fades or dies.

Lifted up is an interesting way of describing the crucifixion. It takes attention away from the pain and shame by elevating Jesus. Jesus spoke of his ordeal as his glory.

The second explanation asserts God's love for the world. The One who has painstakingly created a thing wants it to work. St Paul wrote:

> But now, freed from the commands of sin
> and bound to the service of God, you have
> gains that lead to holiness, and the end is
> eternal life.
> (Romans 6:22)

The third explanation brings to mind a court case, a guilty verdict and prison. Jesus did not come to be a judge or to punish, but as a rescuer.

In the fourth explanation the believer is forgiven. The case against them is closed. Faith in Jesus bypasses judgement. The person who opts to stay with the evil one judges themselves; turning away from the light of Jesus keeps the case open.

The fifth explanation ends: those who live by the truth come to the light so that it may be clearly seen that God is in all they do.

That is a beautiful description of the christian life—what it is, and its witness.

We underestimate the effect of darkness on our lives. It's tentacles extend deeply and far. They touch a multitude of things, to spoil them.

Children of light reflect God's light, away from themselves into the world.

People see value in that, although they are reluctant to give up what grips them, in order to move into the light. Jesus told a parable about a king who called a wedding feast, but the guests did not come. Jesus ended the parable:

> For many are invited, but few are chosen.
> (Matthew 22:24)

THE SHEPHERD AND
THE GARDENER

JESUS DESCRIBED HIMSELF AS THE GOOD SHEPHERD, WHO
looks after and protects his sheep. He told a parable which
depicted God as a gardener. The two together show how Jesus
and God impinge on us as christians, tended by the Son and
by the Father.

Followers of Jesus are sometimes referred to as *the flock*.
Unlike goats, which go their own ways exploring, sheep tend to
keep together in a flock; should one wander off, the rest follow.

The concept of the good shepherd comes in the old
testament in Psalm 23.

> The Lord is my shepherd; I lack for nothing.
> He makes me lie down in green pastures,
> he leads me to water where I may rest;
> he revives my spirit;
> for his name's sake he guides me in the right
> paths.
> (Psalm 23:1–3)

Here comes the idea of being moved along and guided;
the Lord moves his flock so that our needs are well met and

we progress the way we should. The Lord sees to our present and to our future, not forgetting our need to be sometimes revived.

It can be helpful to look back over episodes of one's life, to note the Lord's hand along the path to where one has got to now.

The psalm goes on to comment that in the dark valleys of life we have no fear of harm, we feel protected. That is our experience as we follow Jesus.

The second stanza speaks of a table of provisions set for us, a rich anointing and our cup of life full to the brim and running over. Psalm 23 ends:

> Goodness and love unfailing will follow me
> all the days of my life,
> and I shall dwell in the house of the Lord
> throughout the years to come.
> (Psalm 23:6)

Many christians find comfort in Psalm 23. We go through life protected by God's love. God's love gives us a good life. Jesus' life was one of service, service to God and to man. That is the life in which the good shepherd leads us; to take pleasure in serving.

The word *flock* is an apt description. Besides being together, believers have a common understanding between us. A third thing is that we are going in the same direction, in fact to the same destination. We have the same purpose, to serve God and love our neighbour. As we do God's work we are aware of his hand in big things and in little things, in things that just come out.

> This is why I tell you not to be anxious about
> food and drink ... and about clothes to cover
> your body ... Look at the birds in the sky;
> they do not sow and reap and store in barns,
> yet your heavenly Father feeds them.
> (Matthew 6:25–26)

Jesus knows us. He looks after us. In the end there will be one flock, one shepherd, one Kingdom.

> I am the good shepherd; I know my own
> and my own know me ... But there are other
> sheep of mine, not belonging to this fold;
> I must lead them as well, and they too will
> listen to my voice. There will then be one
> flock, one shepherd.
> (John 10:14–16)

Jesus warned of two dangers to the flock: the thief and the wolf. The thief steals. Satan uses many ploys to seduce us away from living as Jesus said. The wolf ravages the flock. Little things keep people running around all day, no time for God.

When we decide to follow Jesus we make ourselves a target for Satan. As long as we listen to the voice of Jesus, we are guarded from Satan's attacks.

In the other illustration Jesus described himself as the stem of a vine, which supports and nourishes us, the branches. Father God is the gardener.

> I am the true vine, and my Father is the
> gardener. Any branch of mine that is barren

> he cuts away; and any fruiting branch he
> prunes clean, to make it more fruitful still. ...
> No branch can bear fruit by itself, but only
> if it remains united with the vine; no more
> can you bear fruit, unless you remain united
> with me.
> (John 15:1–4)

First we note that branches that do not play their part are cut off. They are left to wither away.

The other branches are pruned, so as to improve them. That is another side of God's dealing with us, one which is often neglected. When something is cut off from our life we should see if God is behind it. We should willingly accept being pruned, knowing that it is for our good and the accomplishment of God's purpose.

God's Kingdom is fruitful. We are shaped to that end. We should see our place in the world and God's dealings with us in that way.

St Paul wrote about our place in the church. We should think of our place in the Kingdom similarly.

> And it is he who has given some to be
> apostles, some prophets, some evangelists,
> some pastors and teachers, to equip God's
> people for work in his service, for the
> building up of the body of Christ...
> (Ephesians 4:11–13)

A GOOD LIFE

HOW DO I BUILD MYSELF A GOOD LIFE? THAT IS NOT A
profitable question. It is God who builds. The best life is when
God forms it.

God creates each person with qualities and abilities which
the world around us needs. We should just be ourself, our true
self. Then the gifts with which the Lord has endowed us flow
out naturally. The natural flow towards our neighbours costs us
nothing. It uplifts them. It leads us to feel fulfilled. That is our joy.

> The Lord has told you mortals what is good,
> and what it is that the Lord requires of you:
> only to act justly, to love loyalty,
> to walk humbly with your God.
> (Micah 6:8)

The word translated *loyalty* is, in the hebrew, *hésed*.
Hésed is a broad concept, like *shalom*. Other translations are
mercy, loving kindness. We need to combine them all to absorb
the full meaning.

The text points us to humility. St Paul also pointed his
christians to humility, and to looking to each other's interests.
Both build people together.

> Leave no room for selfish ambition and
> vanity, but humbly reckon others better than
> yourselves. Look to each other's interests
> and not merely to your own.
> (Philippians 2:3–4)

We should keep God in mind all the time. That gives us a reference point outside ourself.

We should also cogitate on what Jesus taught, to really get into it and do it. Our love to Jesus is not a feeling. It is following him. Jesus gave us a double promise: he would love us and he would disclose himself to us. It had a condition.

> Anyone who has received my commands
> and obeys them–he it is who loves me; and
> he who loves me will be loved by my Father;
> and I will love him and disclose myself
> to him.
> (John 14:21)

All that Jesus said and did was in consultation with his Father through prayer. We too have prayer, and also the Holy Spirit. We know God, we just share our life with him.

Jesus suggested going to a quiet corner to pray. From time to time he went right away, up a mountain or into the wilderness. For us a retreat is an uplifting experience, be it alone or with a group.

Sometimes we need a quick decision: what am I to say to that? That is a time for a quick prayer, even one silent word, 'help!'. Jesus warned against talking too much. We need to listen.

> In your prayers do not go babbling on like
> the heathen ... for your Father knows what
> your needs are before you ask him.
> (Matthew 6;7–8)

The disciples asked Jesus to teach them how to pray. They had not really got the idea. Jesus had not thought of doing that; prayer was to come naturally. Nonetheless Jesus gave them the Lord's Prayer. The Bible has two versions of it: Matthew 4:9–13 and Luke 11:2–4.

Prayers from a prayer book may put what we want to say better than we can. We want to word our prayers well. What is on our heart to say is the real thing, rather than what books give us to say.

We should beware of making God our servant; he is the supreme architect who organises his creation to run smoothly. He is not a magic button in our pocket.

We have seen that a great deal that Jesus taught was about relating to other people. Some people do that naturally and others less so. The Lord has made each one of us an individual. But, however we are, we all need a basis for our lives and an environment into which we fit and feel a part.

If one sees a person looking sad or unhappy, one can pray for them, there and then. Ask God whether to speak to them, and, if so, what to say.

When conversing, we can quietly mention God or the church. Surprisingly often, that is taken up; the other person is open to talk. From a small comment we drop out, God opens a door through us. We have to make the comment for it to happen.

Chapter 21 of the Gospel of St Matthew records a parable which Jesus told about two sons. Their father had a job to be done in his vineyard and asked the sons to do it. One said, 'Yes, sir', but did not go. The other said, 'I won't'. But he had second thoughts and went and did the job. Jesus asked, which son did what his father wanted?

The essential thing is not to look for things to do for the Lord, but to be available when the Lord needs us. If the Lord sees us as reliable, then he may call upon us more. He may send people to us.

We may apply the parable of the two sons to ourselves in another way. Whatever we once said about God and his Kingdom, what counts is what we do in the end.

We try not to do wrong. One wrong thing throws other things out. Our escape hatch is repentance. To repent is not to apologise. It is a deep, personal thing, between me and God. It is to acknowledge the wrong, hate it, turn away from it, and resolve never ever to let it happen again. God honours that. He gives forgiveness, a way out and a way on. Over and above that, repentance gives peace. It heals a wound, stops it from festering.

We should always forgive anyone who injures us or hurts our feelings. They may feel bad about it. It can stay in their mind and ours for years.

The person who says, 'I cannot forgive that' is inviting Satan to rule their life.

St Paul observed that there are people who have the Lord's way written in their hearts. They naturally do what is right in the Lord's eyes.

> None will be justified before God by hearing
> the law, but by doing it. When Gentiles who
> do not possess the law carry out its precepts

> by the light of nature ... they show that
> what the law requires is inscribed on their
> hearts...
> (Romans 2:13–15)

Jesus aimed for everyone to be like that. It will come, as our circle matures and expands in Jesus.

The remarkable thing about Jesus is that, the deeper and deeper we dig into his teaching, the more and more we discover about him and about life and about ourselves.

Today's world is unsatisfactory. Jesus is the Way to the Truth which brings back Life, brings us and God together.

> Come for water, all who are thirsty;
> though you have no money, come, buy grain
> and eat...
> Why spend your money for what is not food,
> your earnings on what fails to satisfy?
> Listen to me and you will fare well,
> you will enjoy the fat of the land.
> (Isaiah 55:1–2)

There is much else that Jesus did.
If it were all to be recorded in detail,
I suppose the world could not hold
the books that would be written.
(John 21:24–25)

OTHER BOOKS BY JIM PRESTIDGE

Weekly Prayers around the Bible
ISBN 978-1-9736-8842-6

The Gospel of the Kingdom
Seven Bible studies
ISBN 978-1-6642-0272-6

Jesus Said
A study of the teaching of Jesus
ISBN 978-1-6642-3597-7

Prayer for Tomorrow's World
ISBN: 978-1-6642-5480-0
Bible studies for groups or individuals

Day by day
Let's get to know Jesus a little bit more
Christianity explained to a child
ISBN: 978-1-6642-5963-8